# Fuck Off

## I'm Coloring

# Dicks

# This Book Belongs To:

______________________________

## Cock Coloring Book For Adults

# Disclaimer

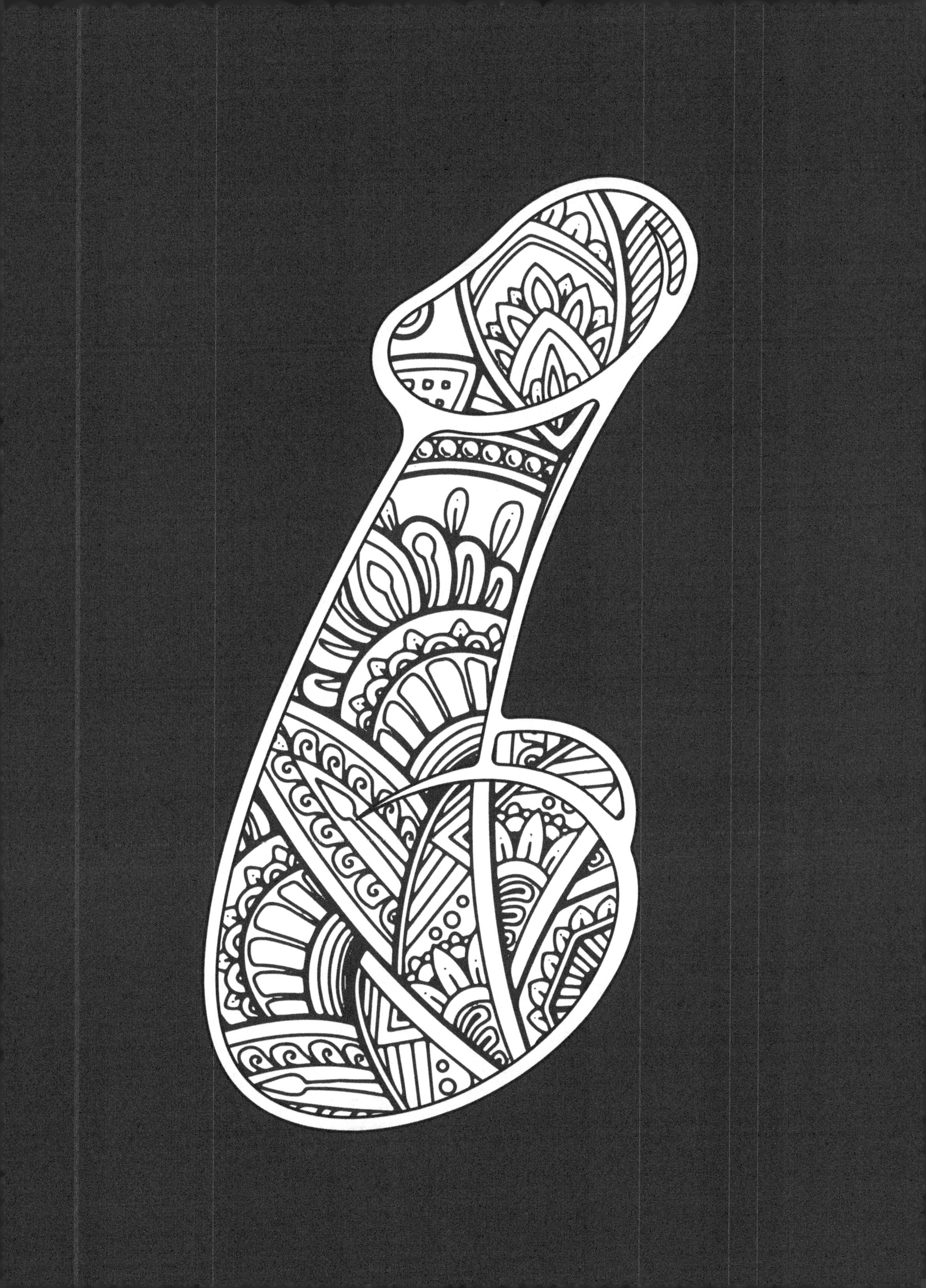

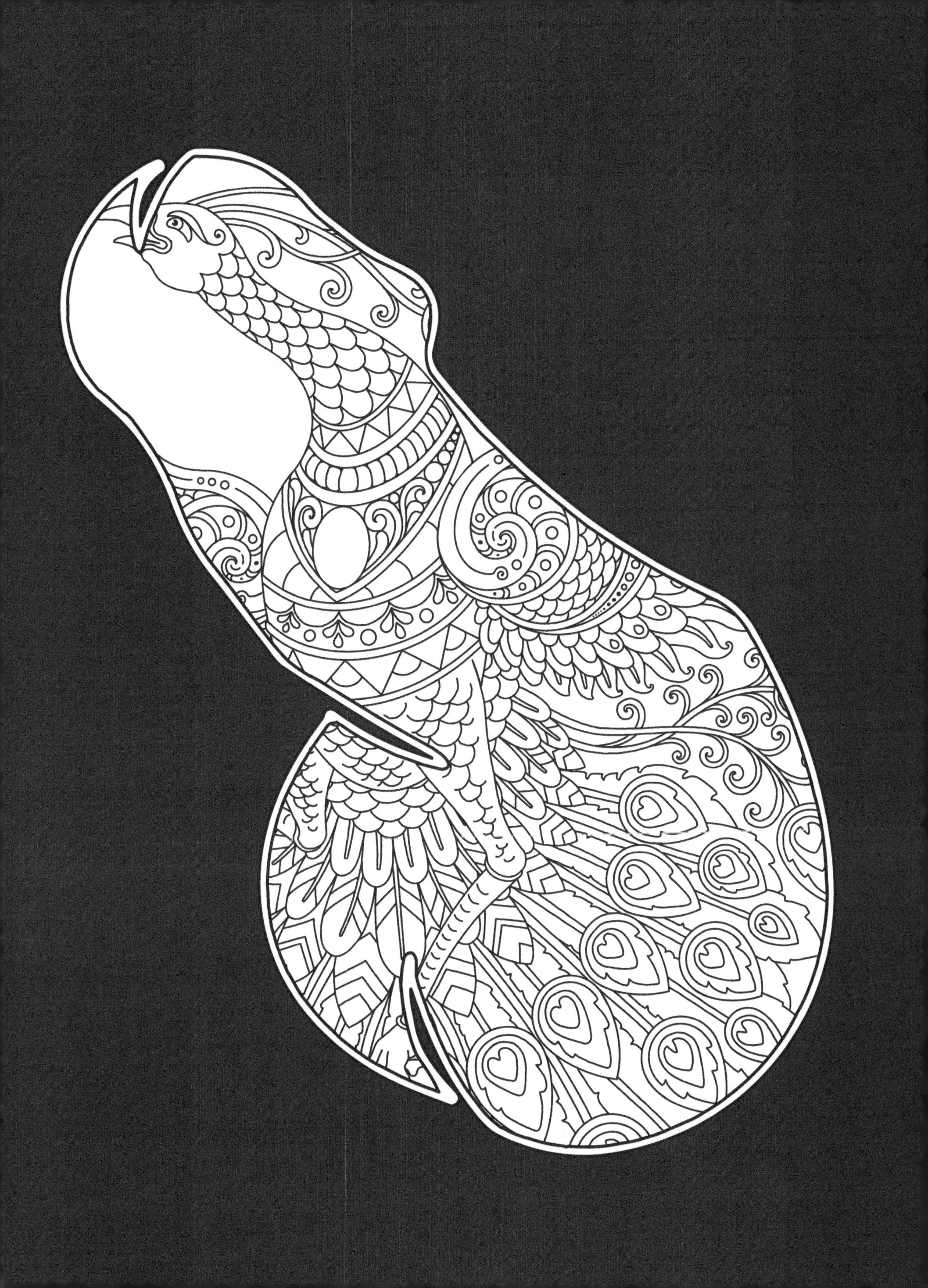

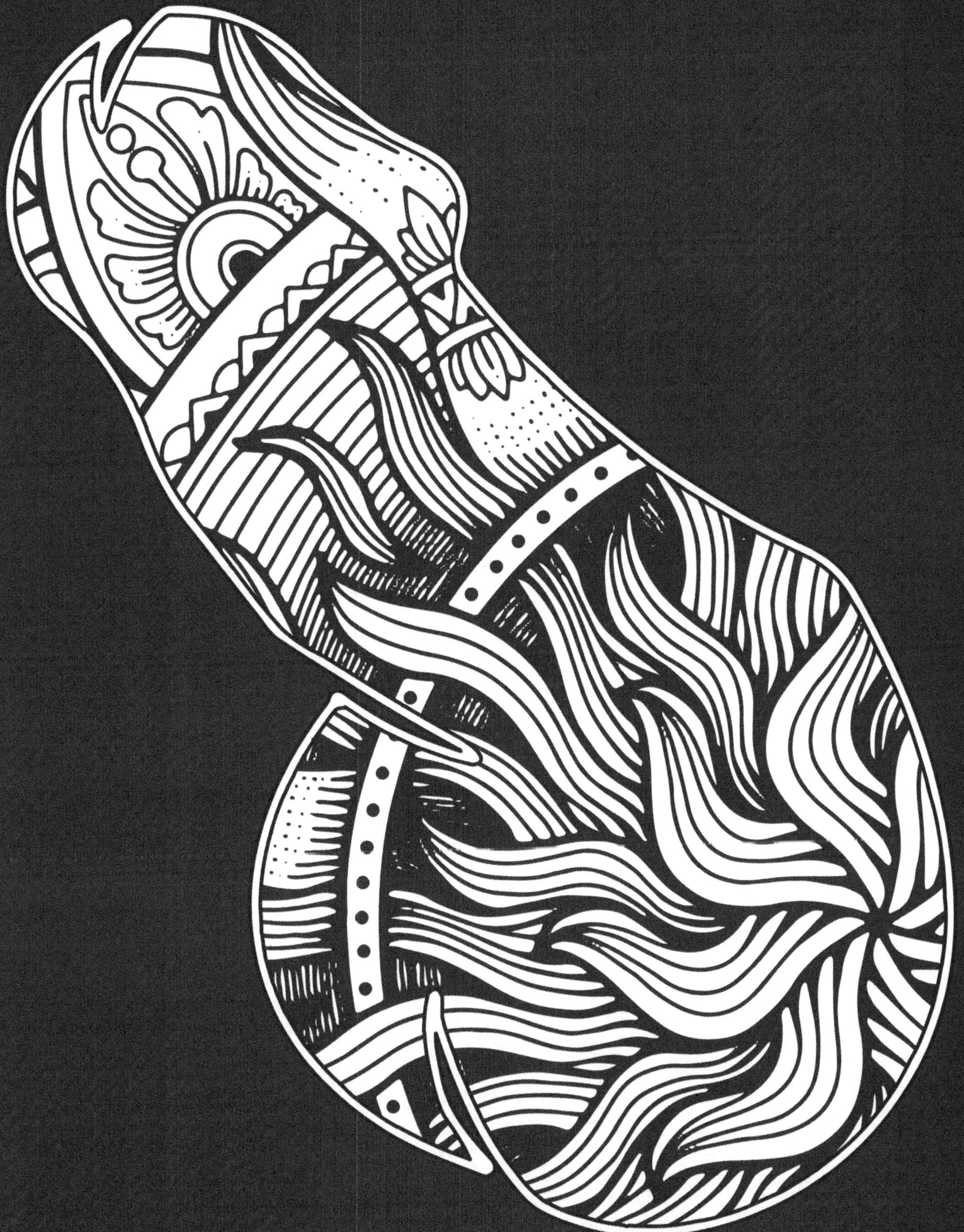

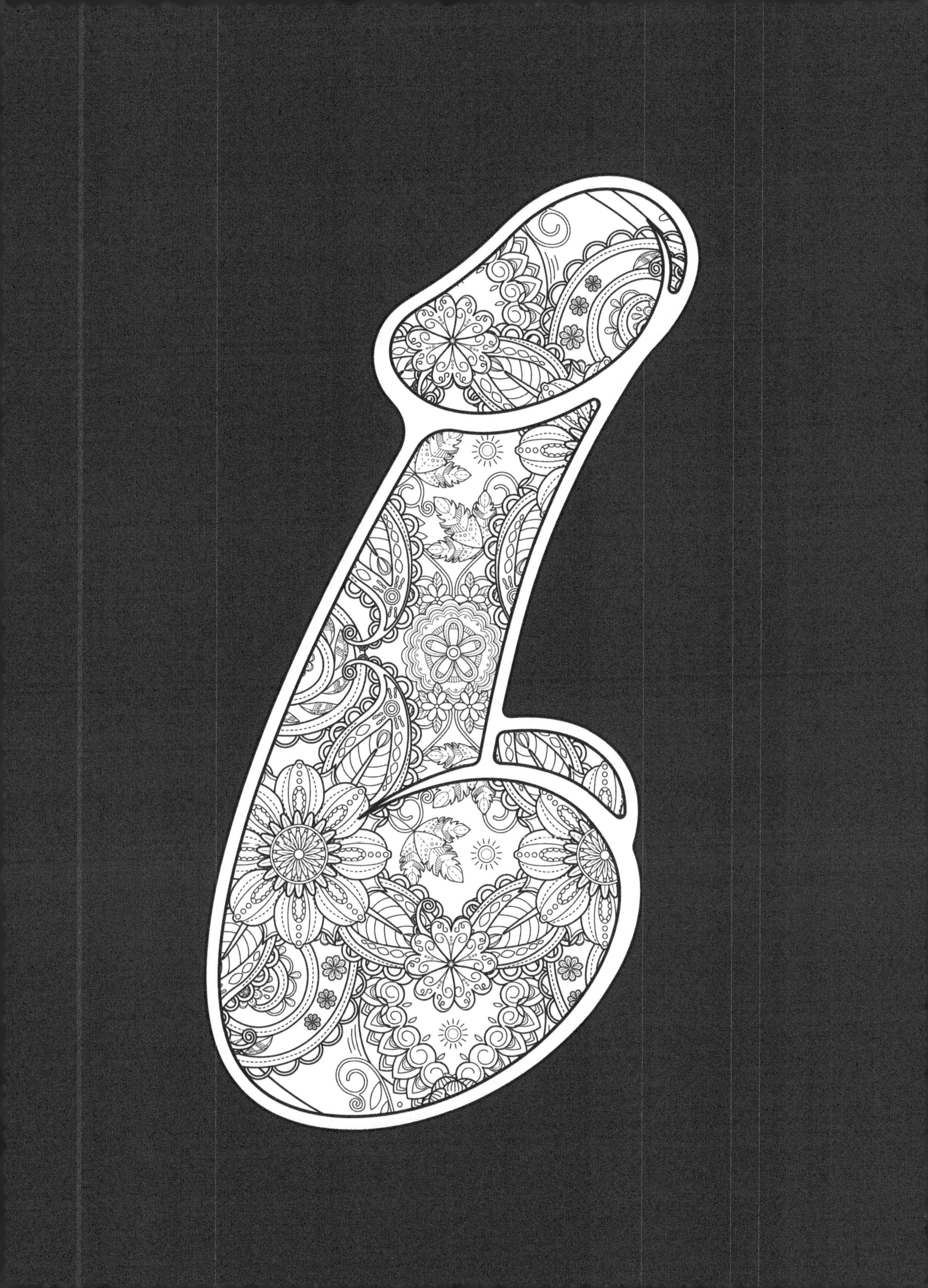

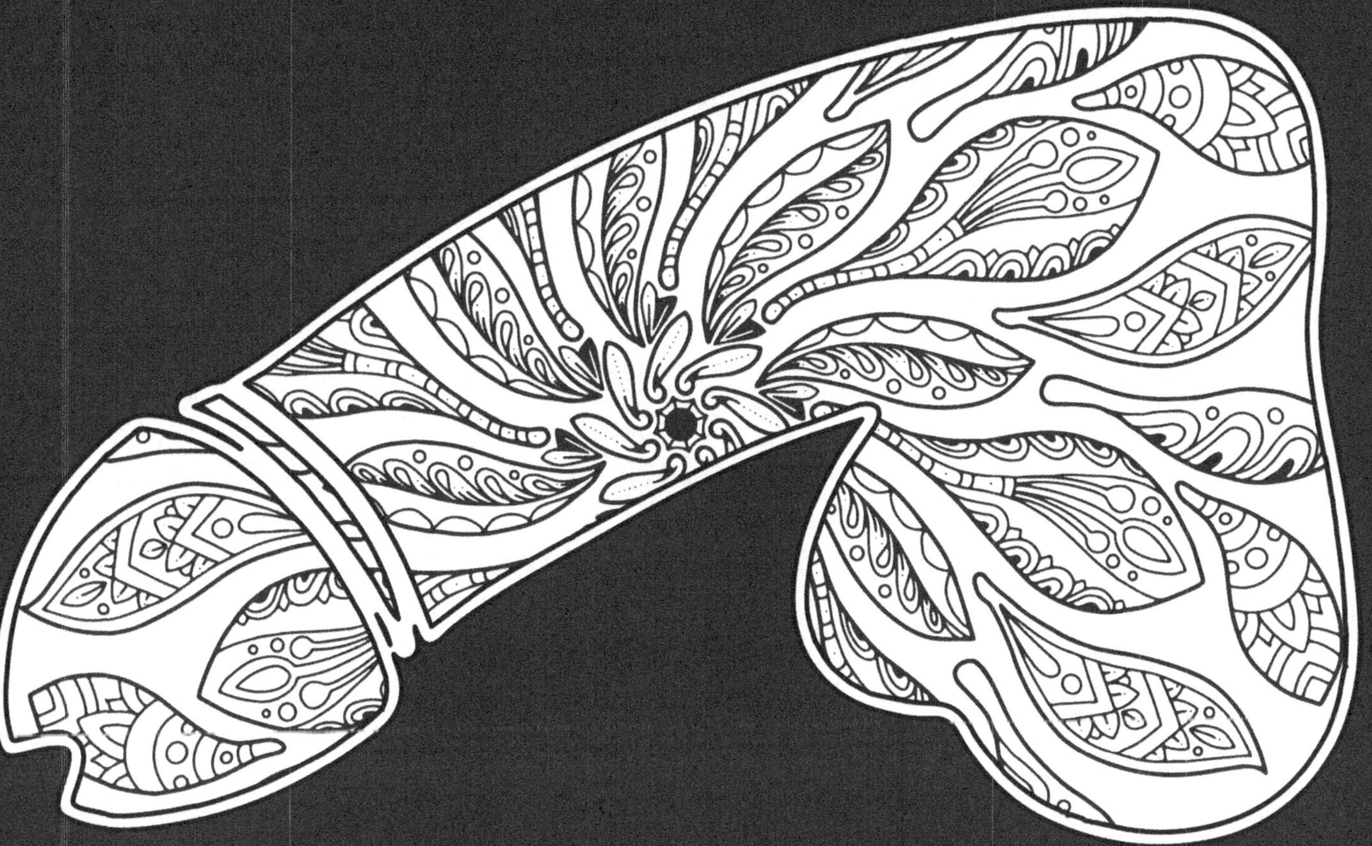

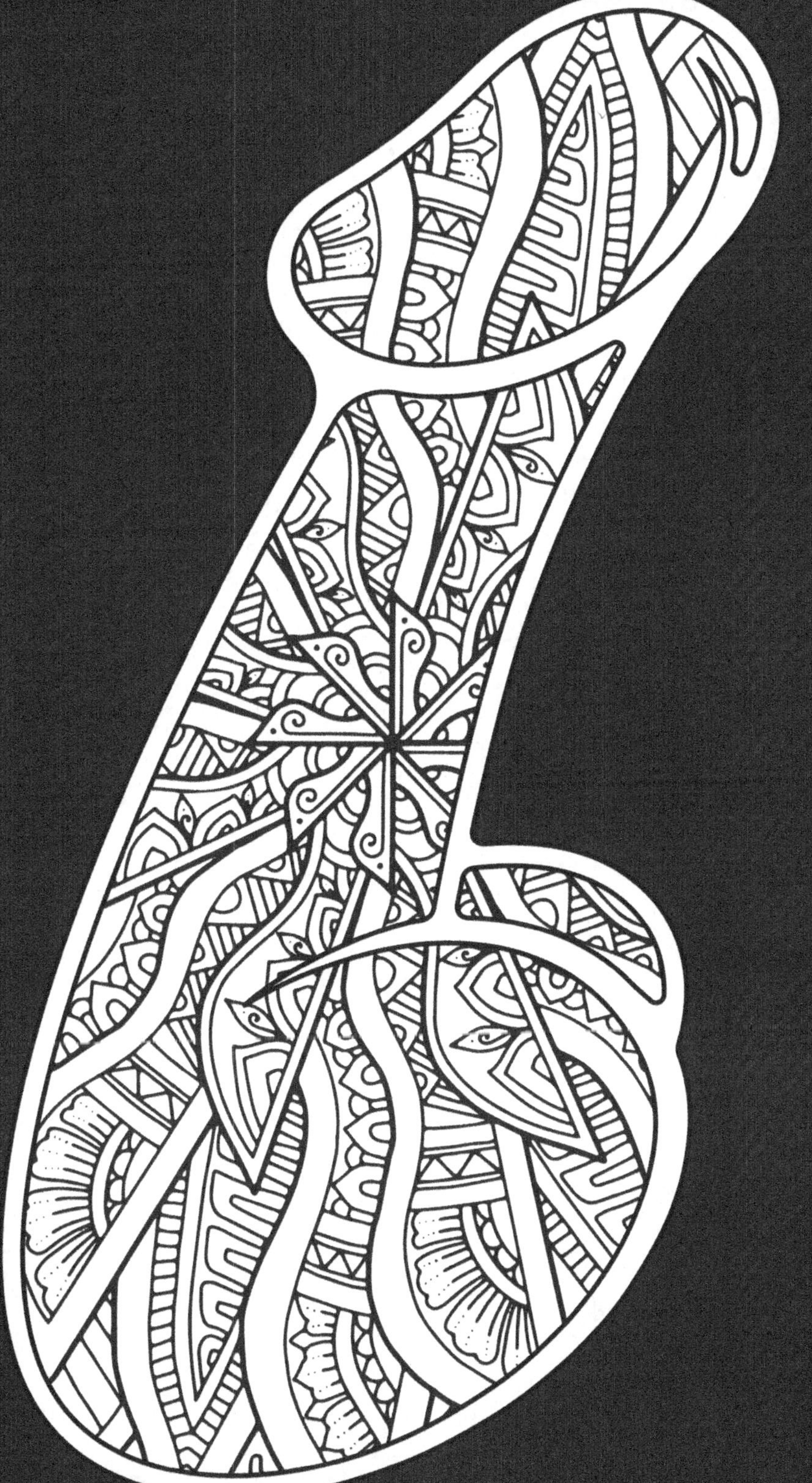

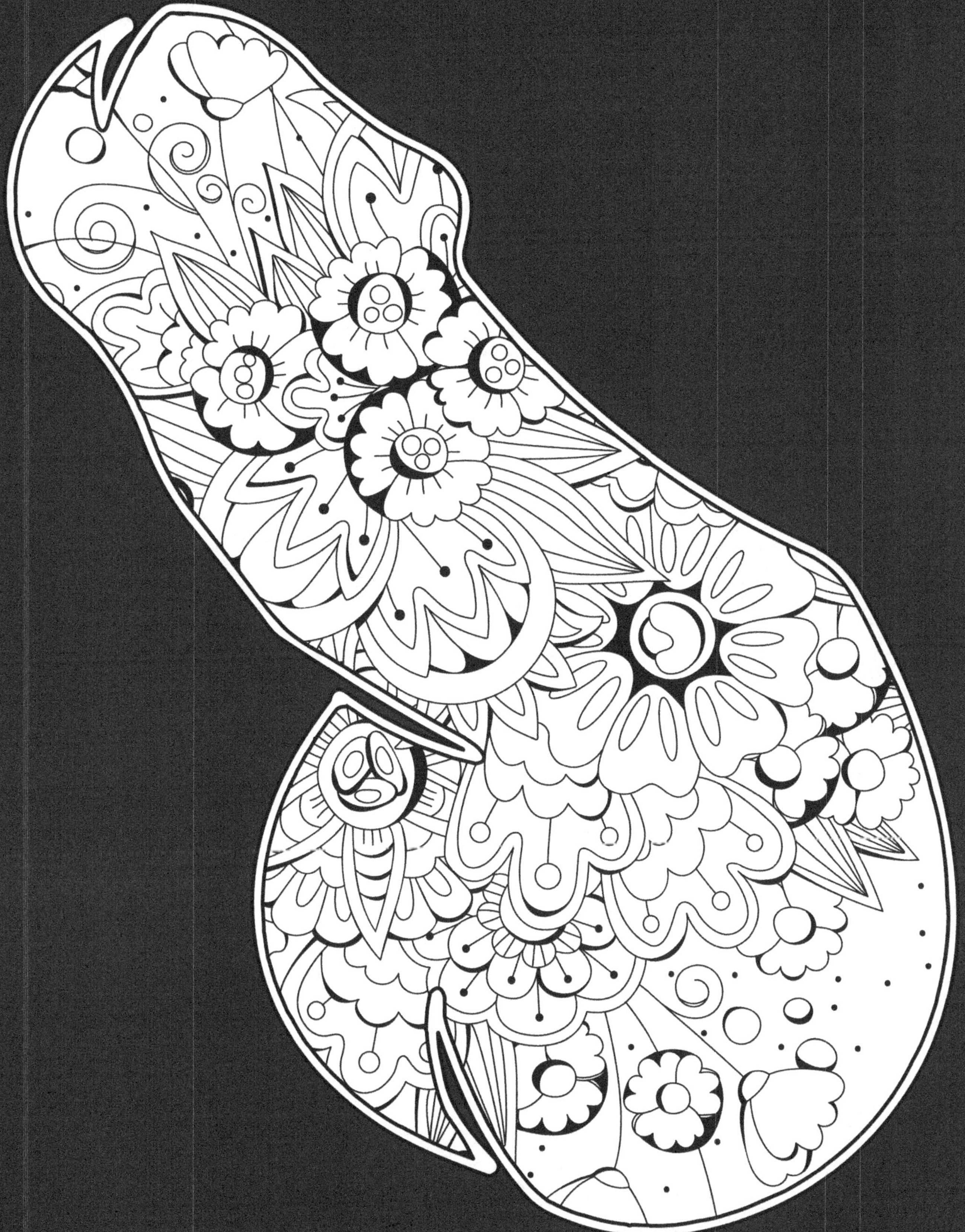

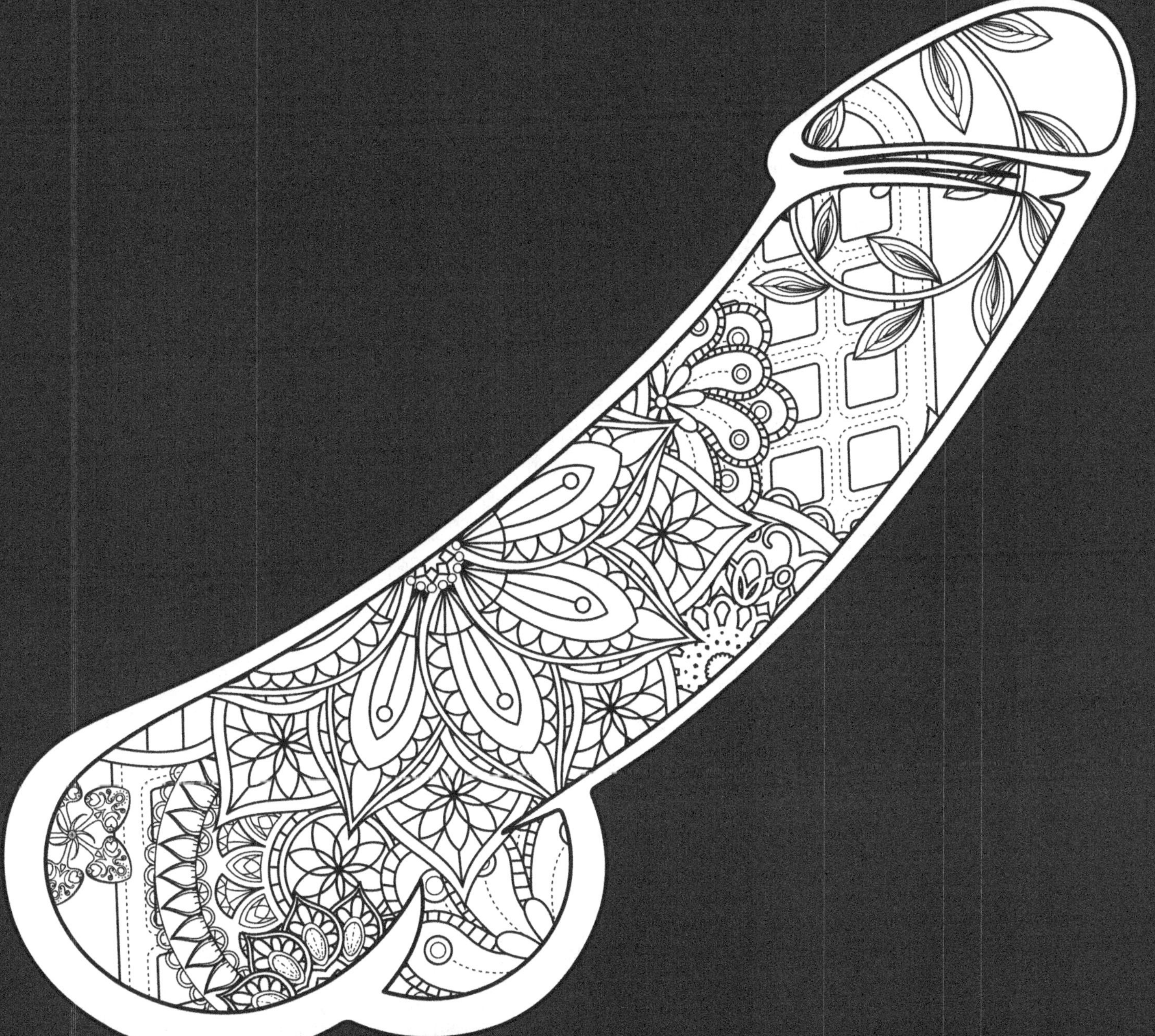

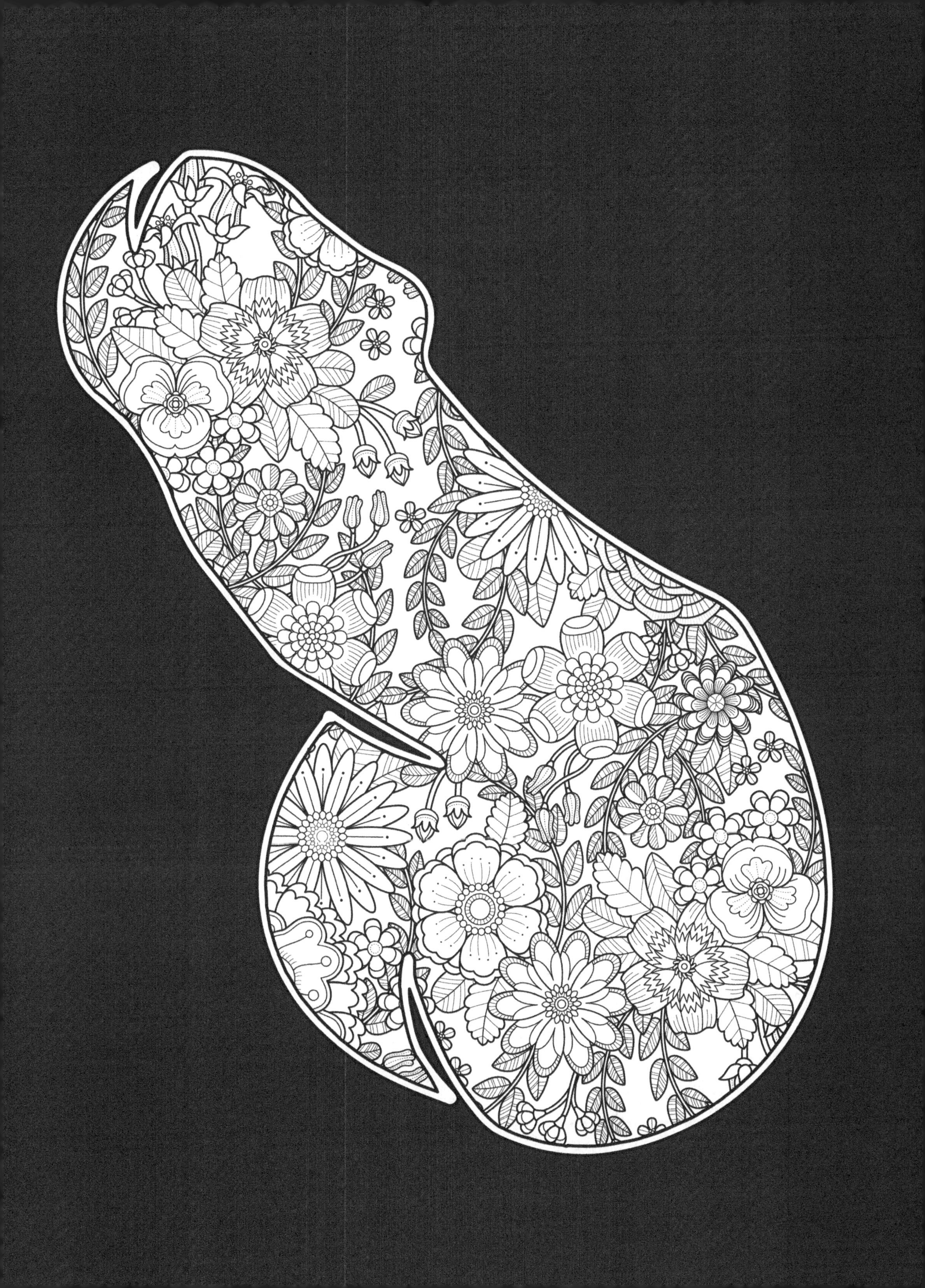

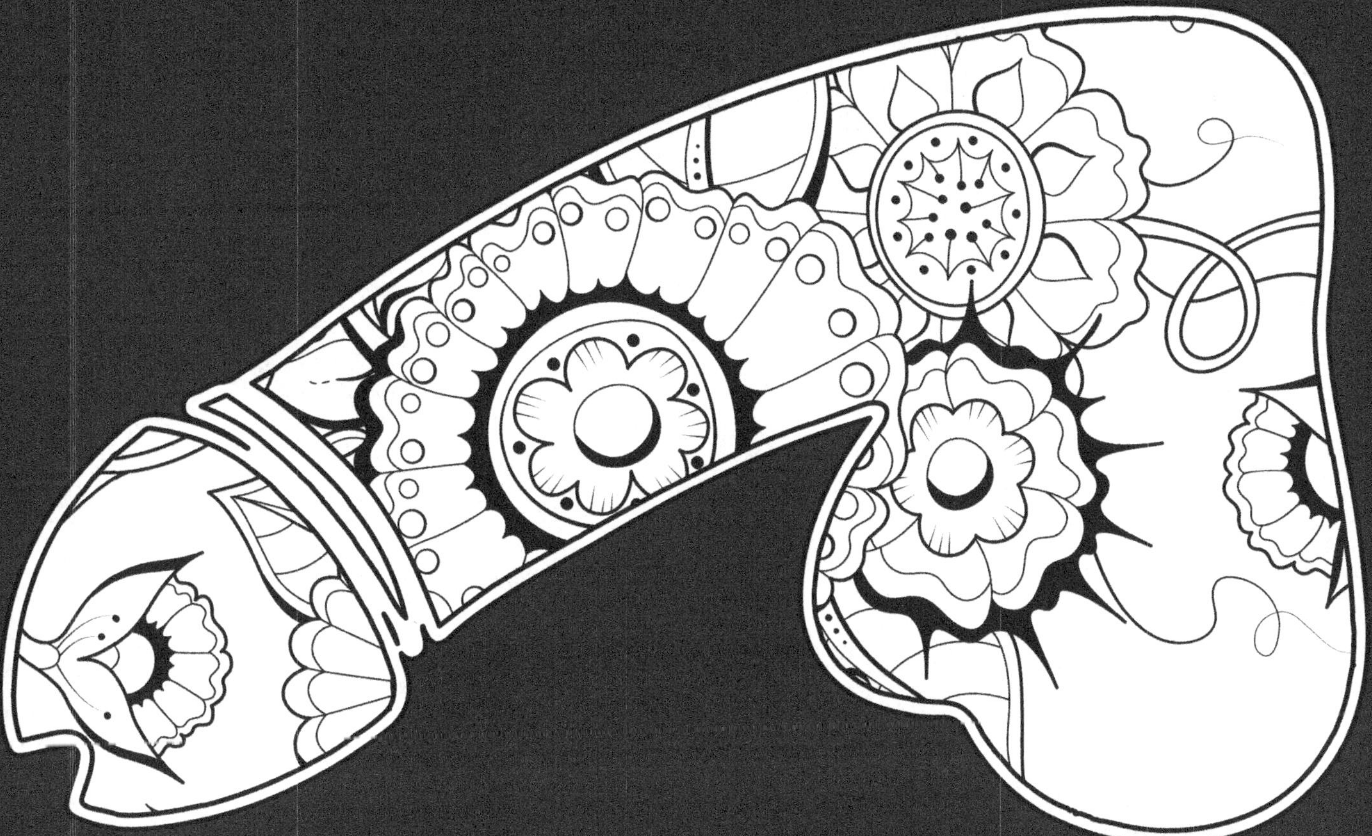

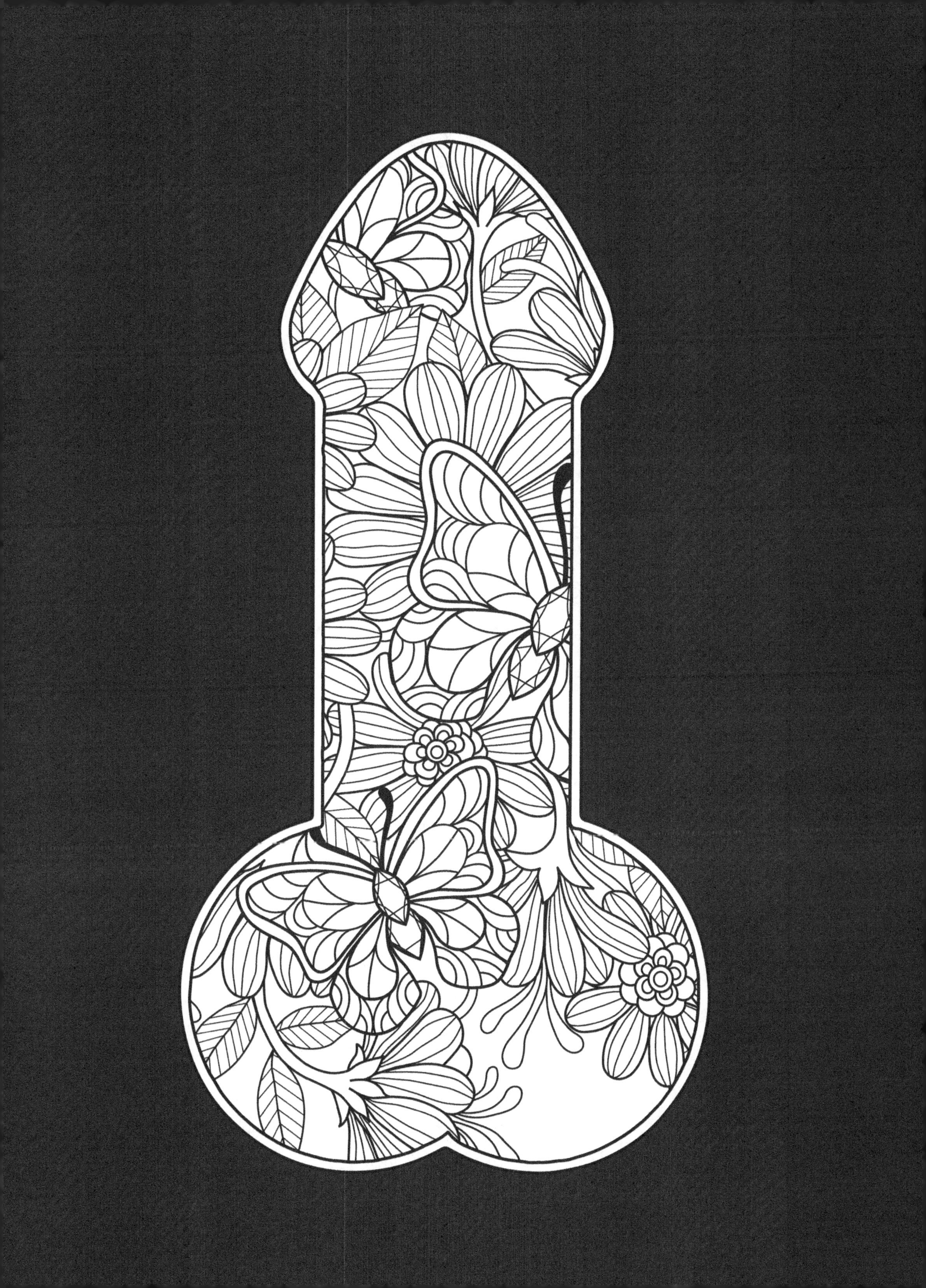

Made in the USA
Las Vegas, NV
27 November 2024

12758292R00059